Night
Adoration at
the Home

Father Mateo
Crawley-Boevey, SS.CC.

SENSUS FIDELIUM PRESS

Gastonia, North Carolina

Contents

Letters From Pius XI to Fr. Mateo

L ETTERS FROM HIS HOLINESS, PIUS XI
TO FATHER MATEO

The Vatican, April 4, 1929

Most Reverend Father,

The Sovereign Pontiff gladly received the letters in which so many bishops give their approbation to the work of Nocturnal Adoration. These letters, coming from you as a homage on behalf of all the Night Adorers, and on the occasion of His Jubilee, have given Him the greatest pleasure.

His Holiness cordially thanks you for this fresh testimony of the veneration felt for His Sacred

Person. He sees in it yet another mark of the zeal for souls which animates you, and of your devotedness to the social duty of making reparation for the many outrages offered to our Lord, Who loves men so much, and yet is not loved in return.

Having noted with great satisfaction the good results of this apostolate the Sovereign Pontiff blesses it wholeheartedly. In the belief that it will help much toward enabling many souls to live in true accord with the teaching of the holy Gospels, He sends as a pledge of His Fatherly interest, to you and to ALL NOCTURNAL ADORERS, A SPECIAL APOSTOLIC BLESSING.

Accept, Reverend Father, the assurance of my own devotedness in your regard.

(Signed) CARD. GASPARRI

The Vatican, October 25, 1930

Reverend Father,

His Holiness has entrusted to me the pleasant duty of requesting you to thank on His behalf all Nocturnal Adorers in the Home for the rich treasure of so many nights of prayer offered as a mark of filial affection on the occasion of His Sacerdotal Jubilee.

The Holy Father is happy to express His best wishes for the success of this work of reparation, which will undoubtedly be productive of the most consoling results. He imparts most lovingly to all the members, as a token of His Fatherly benevolence, the Apostolic Benediction.

Believe me, Reverend Father,

Yours devotedly in Jesus Christ,

(Signed) E. CARD. PACELLI

Night Adoration
in the Home
Comments

Night Adoration in the Home is now, thanks be to God, a fact, a magnificent reality. It is a work solidly organized throughout the entire world in a spirit of love and penance, for the honor and glory of the Heart of Jesus. May the King of Love be blessed a thousand times for it! To Him, and to Him alone, be all the glory of this crusade of Night Adoration which, while strengthening His Social Reign, especially in the home, gives a new and vigorous impulse for the extension of that Reign.

From all parts requests have come to us for a "Holy Hour" for the use of Night Adorers in the Home, as there are many who feel the need of being guided in an exercise of piety which has, in truth, a special character and a spirit all its own.

We respond gladly therefore by offering to the thousands of Nocturnal Adorers their own "Holy Hour." It is dictated and inspired by the same sentiments which gave birth to this great work of reparation, namely: the heartbreaking and appalling spectacle of an unheard-of laxity among Christians in our day; the tremendous offense which prevails in social customs, theatres and feminine fashions; and the culpable worldliness of a great number of Catholics who live in open rebellion against the laws of God and the admonitions and commands of the Sovereign Pontiff.

Ah yes, the Heart of Jesus is "sad even unto death," feeling His pierced side reopened, mortally wounded, by many of those who by right ought to be His intimate friends but who are in fact His executioners. A perfidy that is a sacrilegious cruelty; a cruelty that is treachery!

May this beautiful practice of the Nocturnal Holy Hour have the power of provoking the reaction which can come by no other means! And we hope that with its supernatural element of penance, of love and of adoration, it may be able to appease the Divine Justice, which, unless we make reparation, must needs punish the guilty with great rigor. The world truly is preparing a cataclysm.

We are, in fact, on the brink of an abyss of social corruption: the home already undermined in its very foundations by this upheaval of immorality; a good part of that portion of society which by right is considered the best, the most Christian, seriously affected by the contagion of unbridled sensuality; the woman who thinks herself good and even devout, dressed in a style not only immodest but scandalous, dancing, conversing and amusing herself in a manner that would imply she had never been baptized. In her worldly-mindedness she will even smile with the air of a pagan when the Pope or Bishop condemns these excesses, preaching modesty of dress and chastity of heart and of social life.

And the young girl who scarcely a few years ago was as a lily for the altar of Mary Immaculate, is caught today in the giddy whirl of pleasure and passion, to fall, alas, a withered flower; in the course of a short time, under the pressure of the worldly current, she is talking and dressing in an indecent fashion like everybody else, yet she still calls herself a "Child of Mary." What a mockery!

The Virgin Most Pure indeed becomes the Mother of Sorrows when she beholds this garden of youthful souls devastated in the very morning of life, blighted by the poisonous, impure breath of our modern society. Lilies and violets which of old were treasured as symbols of purity, of humility and of womanly dignity, have — alas, for the disgrace of it! — lost their meaning for Christians of this age —Christians who do not preserve by so much as a sign the character of Baptism, much less its rich and beautiful heritage, for of that the whole perverse world has sacrilegiously robbed our Lord.

Penance, prayer and satisfaction! If we follow any other road we shall perish miserably, inasmuch as God is just and holy. Yes, we shall perish, for the guilty are really responsible: they know what they are doing.

May the mercy of the Sacred Heart fill up the immense abyss made by so many crimes and sins, by so many scandals. Let us pray, let us do penance, let us make reparation.

JESUS, MERCY!

Remember this was published August 7, 1944. Things have gotten much worse today!

Practical Suggestions

T his monthly hour of Night Adoration, as you already know, is made at home. In large families the adoration may be arranged in such a way that each member of the family watches in turn before a picture of the Sacred Heart. If the Sacred Heart has been enthroned in the home, then the adoration should take place before the enthroned picture of the Sacred Heart, around which lighted candles and flowers have been placed, if this is possible and practical. The hours are assigned to each member of the family by the father or mother. If the family is large enough (nine members) then the adoration may begin at nine and continue until six; in smaller families it may begin at nine and continue until all the members of the family have made their hour of adoration. At the end of each hour the next adorer is called by the preceding one. If it is not practical to make the adoration as described above, then the entire family may make it together at a determined hour. Again the father and mother may desire to make it together or singly. In this case the adoration may be made in the privacy of one's room. The family is free to arrange this matter according to circumstances, If the family makes adoration at the same hour, the father or mother or even one of the older children might lead the prayers and the others in the responses, as is done during a Holy Hour in church.

The adoration should be made as far as possible on one's knees, in a spirit of salutary penance — otherwise one should kneel for at least a few moments at the beginning and again at the end of the hour. It should be throughout a Eucharistic Adoration, in spirit and in truth. Picture to yourself the walls of His sacramental prison, and contemplate our King and Prisoner of Love in the complete solitude and abandonment of the tabernacle; in this

Gethsemane He will be consoled by the chalice of sweetness offered to Him by the adoring soul.

It would be helpful to hold a crucifix in your hands and to press it with love, while reading and pondering the considerations and prayers of this Holy Hour. Read slowly, read with immense love, prompted more by your heart than by mine, that you may be able to realize something of the anguish of our crucified God. Interrupt the reading now and then to meditate on whatever touches your heart, to linger with delight over some idea or ejaculation, such as an expression of contrition, of love, of fidelity.

I suggest that you pray for the following intentions during your hour of adoration: our Holy Father the Pope, peace, the clergy, the members of your family who may have gone astray, those in their agony this night, the Social Reign of the Sacred Heart, particularly through the Enthronement of the Sacred Heart in the Home.

Oh, be true angels of Gethsemane in this Nocturnal Adoration, you who have an advantage over the angel from Heaven, since you are able to suffer and to weep in union with the agonizing Heart of Jesus.

Turn to our Lady of Sorrows, grieve in company with this Mother of bitter woe with whom you now assist at a passion which is lasting through the ages; think that the sword which pierces her Immaculate Heart nowadays is, above all, the worldly frivolity of women, their lack of modesty and of purity.

Finally, remember that this homage of reparation, which is the hour of Night Adoration, is the very same which the Sacred Heart asked of St. Margaret Mary. In union, then, with His confidant and apostle of Paray-le-Monial, gather up in the chalice of a contrite and loving heart all the tears and the countless griefs of our Saviour, that in this hour of intimacy you may soothe His dreadful agony.

And be assured of this, adoring souls: you are making ready now in the best possible way for the hour of your own agony. Oh, with what peace and joy you will then be able to meet this Divine King, most faithful and grateful, Who in your last moments will offer you His own Heart as a refuge! You shall die in His arms, and in your agony He will hold you close to the Precious Wound in His side, in return for the consolation which you have offered to Him hundreds of times in your Night Adoration. And dying thus, you will enter through the portals of the Sacred Heart into Paradise.

Father Mateo urges all Night Adorers to begin their hour of adoration by reading the Canon of the Mass — adoring, praising, petitioning and atoning "THROUGH HIM, WITH HIM, AND IN HIM."

The Canon of
the Mass

We therefore humbly pray and beseech Thee, most merciful Father, through Jesus Christ Thy Son, our Lord, that Thou wouldst accept and bless these gifts, these presents, these holy, spotless sacrifices, which in the first place we offer Thee for Thy Holy Catholic Church, to which vouchsafe to grant peace, as also to preserve, unite and govern it throughout the world: together with Thy servant, N., our Pope, and N., our Bishop, as also all orthodox believers and professors of the Catholic and Apostolic Faith.

Be mindful, O Lord, of Thy servants and handmaids, N. and N., and of all here present, whose faith and devotion are known unto Thee; for whom we offer or who offer up to Thee this sacrifice of praise for themselves and all their friends, for the redemption of their souls, for the hope of their salvation and welfare; and who pay their vows to Thee, the eternal, living and true God.

Communicating with and honoring, in the first place, the memory of the glorious and ever-Virgin Mary, the Mother of God and of our Lord Jesus Christ; as also of Thy blessed Apostles and Martyrs, Peter and Paul, Andrew, James, John, Thomas, James, Philip, Bartholomew, Matthew, Simon and Thaddeus, Linus, Cletus, Clement, Xystus, Cornelius, Cyprian, Lawrence, Chrysogonus, John and Paul, Cosmas and Damian, and of all Thy saints: through whose merits and prayers grant that we may be in all things defended by the help of Thy protection. Through the same Christ our Lord. Amen.

We therefore beseech Thee, O Lord, that Thou wouldst graciously accept this oblation of our servitude, as also that of Thy whole family; and dispose our days in Thy peace, and commend that we be preserved from eternal damnation and numbered in the flock of Thine elect. Through Christ our Lord. Amen.

Which oblation do Thou, O God, vouchsafe in all respects to make blessed, approved, ratified, reasonable and acceptable; that it may be made for us the Body and Blood of Thy most beloved Son, Jesus Christ our Lord.

Who the day before He suffered took bread into His holy and venerable hands, and with eyes lifted up toward Heaven, unto Thee, God, His almighty Father, giving thanks to Thee blessed it, broke it, and gave it to His disciples, saying: "Take and eat ye all of this,

FOR THIS IS MY BODY."

In like manner, after He had supped, taking also this excellent chalice into His holy and venerable hands, likewise giving Thee thanks, He blessed it and gave it to His disciples, saying: "Take and drink ye all of this,

FOR THIS IS THE CHALICE OF MY BLOOD OF THE NEW AND ETERNAL TESTAMENT, THE MYSTERY OF FAITH, WHICH SHALL BE SHED FOR YOU AND FOR MANY UNTO THE REMISSION OF SINS.

"As often as ye do these things, ye shall do them in remembrance of Me.

"Wherefore, O Lord, we Thy servants, as also Thy holy people, calling to mind the blessed Passion of the same Christ Thy Son our Lord, His resurrection from hell and glorious ascension into Heaven, offer unto Thy most excellent majesty, of Thy gifts and presents, a pure Host, a holy Host, a spotless Host, the holy Bread of eternal life, and Chalice of everlasting salvation.

Upon which vouchsafe to look with a propitious and serene countenance, and to accept them as Thou wast pleased to accept the gifts of Thy just servant Abel, and the sacrifice of our patriarch Abraham, and that which Thy high priest Melchisedech offered to Thee, a holy sacrifice, a spotless host.

We humbly beseech Thee, almighty God, to command these things to be carried by the hands of Thy holy angel to Thine altar on high, in the sight of Thy divine majesty, that as many as shall partake of the most sacred Body and Blood of Thy Son at this altar, may be filled with every heavenly grace and blessing. Through the same Christ our Lord. Amen.

Be mindful, O Lord, of Thy servants and handmaids, N. and N., who have gone before us with the sign of faith, and sleep the sleep of peace.

To these, O Lord, and to all that rest in Christ, grant, we beseech Thee, a place of refreshment, light and peace. Through the same Christ our Lord. Amen.

Also to us sinners Thy servants, confiding in the multitude of Thy mercies, vouchsafe to grant some part and fellowship with Thy holy apostles and martyrs: with John, Stephen, Matthias, Barnabas, Ignatius, Alexander, Marcellinus, Peter, Felicitas, Perpetua, Agatha, Lucy, Agnes, Cecilia, Anastasia, and with all Thy saints; into whose company we beseech Thee to admit us, not in consideration of our merit, but of Thine own gratuitous pardon. Through Christ our Lord.

By Whom, O Lord, Thou dost always create, sanctify, quicken, bless, and give us all these good things. Through Him, and with Him, and in Him, is to Thee, God the Father Almighty, in the unity of the Holy Ghost, all honor and glory. World without end. Amen.

It is recommended to now make a Spiritual Communion.

Spiritual Communion: My Jesus, I believe that Thou art present in the Blessed Sacrament. I love Thee above all things and I desire Thee in my soul. Since I cannot receive Thee Sacramentally, come at least spiritually into my heart. As though Thou wert already there, I embrace Thee; permit not that I should ever be separated from Thee. Amen.

Considerations
and Prayers

O ne morning during her meditation, St.
Margaret Mary heard in the depths of her
soul a piteous call, full of distress and anguish. It
was Jesus Who, bathed in tears, was knocking with
insistency at the door of her heart; He was pleading
for a shelter of adoration and consolation that would
make amends for a horrible profanation He had just
suffered.

Moaning and covered with blood, Jesus begged for
relief and comfort. He wanted to rest His wounded
Heart on a most faithful, loving heart, for He had
need of pouring out His grief to one who would
understand. And when, in Holy Communion, the
saint offered our Savior her heart as His spouse, Jesus,

as one oppressed and out of breath, hastened into
that haven of peace and consolation; then Margaret
Mary heard Him sigh with relief and give Himself up
to her care, consoled and grateful, like an injured man
whose wound one dresses with gentleness and love
after the merciless blade has been withdrawn.

Adoring soul, happy are you to find yourself
tonight in exactly the same enviable position as
the saintly confidant of Paray! For if it is true
that the glory of the Divine King has spread
and increased, it is none the less true that the
revenge of Satan has unleashed against the Adorable
Master a tempest of sin. What is sadder still, the
enemy has now penetrated into our own ranks;
the wolf is encountered with unheard-of cruelty in
a full sheepfold. More, he is tolerated there, even
encouraged by the cowardice of many friends. Thus
Satan and the world have without pity struck and
scourged their God and Lord. His very bones might
be counted through His wounds, for "there is no
soundness in Him."

In this state He knocks at the door of your heart,
adoring soul. He is cold and hungry, He is in tears;
His tunic is torn — and still more His Sacred Heart

— by ungrateful friends. He knocks, because He hastens to offer pardon and mercy for the guilty even while He begs for Himself the bread of love which so many have refused Him.

He ought, in strict justice, to punish with rigor and consume in the flames of a most just vengeance the unnatural children who profane His law and trample underfoot His Precious Blood. Ah! but He desires to be more Savior than Judge; He is Jesus, and as such He wills to reign by pardoning.

But to be pardoned supposes a Divine Justice satisfied by reparation. And it is just this reparation which He comes to ask of you tonight, that thereby He may offer to many guilty souls infinite mercy in place of eternal torments. How great an honor for you to be able to complete the reparation of Calvary and of the altar, and consequently to be able to save thousands of souls who, if they had died before this your hour of adoration, would have been eternally lost!

These souls form an immortal crown which you are giving tonight to Jesus in reparation for the crown of thorns, and this same crown will one day likewise be yours, since in your sublime vocation as a soul of reparation you have consented to be the companion of Margaret Mary.

Now recollect yourself and with great fervor invoke for a moment the Holy Ghost, imploring the grace to hear with profit the voice of the agonizing Master.

The voice of Jesus, pleading:

Thank you, beloved soul, for this hour of loving companionship which, at the sacrifice of your well-earned repose, you offer to My despised love. I thank you and bless you! You draw near in good time, for My heart is overflowing with bitterness. I will repay this immense consolation by unburdening My griefs to your most faithful heart. Yet, reflect that it is your God and your Lord Who speaks with you — and adore Me!

I speak to you thus with infinite condescension because I am the Son of Mary, My name is Jesus, I am God the Savior!

I know that you come to make reparation for the cruelest of sins — the sin of ungrateful friends, who are altogether the most blameworthy because they know what they do and are the most loaded with favors.

But I desire that before all you would speak to Me, if only for a moment, in petition for those who in outward appearance at least, are the greatest sinners — such as the impious who blaspheme Me, the renegades who betray Me — and who never have anyone to pray for them. Do you have pity on those unhappy souls and pray for them, the only really unhappy ones, since they live without faith, without hope, without love.

And when you have finished this petition I will relate to you in intimacy another agony, oh, much more dolorous! But I wish first of all to receive your supplication in favor of those who have fallen into an abyss and who have no one to hold out to them a saving hand. Do this act of charity for Me and for them. Do not delay; My merciful Heart is listening to you — speak!

The adoring soul:

Heart of my God and my King, am I, a poor unworthy thing, to console Thee? I, a sinner, to make Thee smile through those divine tears of Thine? I, dust and nothingness, to sweeten Thy bitterness? I, so many times ungrateful, to have the privilege of tenderly pouring balm on Thy wounds and, drawing out the thorns, of placing in their stead my soul and the souls of many others? Thank Thee, my Jesus, infinite thanks for such a vocation of privilege and of glory, a vocation which I have never merited. O King of Love, I thank Thee!

Since Thou dost permit it and even request it, accept my poor entreaty in favor of the executioners of Thy Calvary, a supplication which I present to Thee enriched with the tears of Mary Immaculate.

Heart of Jesus, sorrowful unto death at receiving the kiss of the perfidious Judas, pity and mercy for so many other wretched ones who have betrayed and sold Thee for a creature, for position, or for vile money. By the sorrows and the tender compassion of Mary, grant that they may return repentant to Thy fold. Jesus, have mercy. Mercy, Lord, mercy!

Heart of Jesus, sorrowful unto death, covered with opprobrium before the court of Herod and dragged with ignominy before the tribunals of the unjust, pity and pardon for so many of the great ones of the earth who, considering themselves to be wise, take it upon themselves in our day to condemn Thee, and this in order to justify their own offenses and to excuse their sin of pride! By the sorrows and the tender compassion of Mary, grant that they may return repentant to Thy fold. Jesus, have mercy. Mercy, Lord, mercy!

Heart of Jesus, sorrowful unto death, nailed to an infamous gibbet between two criminals, abandoned in death by the good and cursed by those very ones for whom Thou wert dying, have pity on so many great sinners who, loaded with worldly honors, are in reality only unhappy traffickers in sin. Have pity on those who have acquired power and glory at the price of Thy Precious Blood! By the sorrows and the tender compassion of Mary, grant that they may return repentant to Thy fold. Jesus, have mercy. Mercy, Lord, mercy!

O good Jesus, in union with our Holy Father the Pope, I entreat Thee in favor of those who have never known Thee, or who having known Thee but little and wrongly, in their ignorance treat Thee in the same manner as do Thy ruthless enemies. Mercy!

Good Jesus, I pray for the many perverted nations living in hatred of Thy Adorable Person and who, in open rebellion against Thy Holy Church, seek in their fury to destroy it, to bury it beneath its own ruins. Mercy!

Good Jesus, I pray for the many, many followers of various sects who are knowingly in error — self-interested, ambitious, wicked men, who hate Thee, who curse Thy Cross and Thy law which condemns them, and who in their hatred plot to dethrone Thee from the altar and from consciences. Mercy!

Good Jesus, I pray for all those whom, through Thy tears on Calvary, Thou didst contemplate down the ages, for all those to whom Thou didst tenderly offer pardon and mercy when, dying, Thou didst say: "Father, forgive them, for they know not what they do." Mercy!

And good Jesus, divining a desire of Thy compassionate Heart, I confidently beseech Thee for my home, for all those whom Thou hast given to me for my own, and whom, in Thee and for Thee, I ought to love in a Christian manner — yet only in Thee, O King and Friend of Bethany! Thou knowest all these who are dear to me and, knowing all things, Thou art not ignorant that in my home there are great sorrows and cruel shadows. . . . Have pity on them all, most faithful Friend of Bethany, and let this adoration be a full reparation for them and for me. I confide to Thy most loving Sacred Heart all the sadness and moral suffering, all the bitterness and anguish of death, that are and will be in my home, which is Thine also, O Jesus.

Alas, Lord, all my dear ones are not yet entirely Thine, as Thou dost desire them to be and, as Lord and King, hast the right to demand. . .. Have pity on them, Divine Friend of Bethany!

Convert, heal and bring to life again, O Heart of Jesus, all those who are living dead in sin round about me, and whom I consecrate to Thee for Thy glory. Enlighten, strengthen and guide them, Thou Who art the Light, Thou Who art Strength, Thou Who art Love!

O Jesus, save and sanctify the family from which Thou hast deigned to choose this adoring lamp, himself (herself) poor and insignificant, but longing to see Thee known, adored and loved without measure in this home. Pity and mercy for us all! Divine Friend of Bethany, may Thy Kingdom come among us!

Make known with all simplicity and confidence the pressing needs of your family: the conversions, the graces of greater fervor, divine light and consolation, etc. Then, with your arms extended in the form of a cross say five Our Fathers, Hail Marys and Glory Be to the Fathers in reparation for all the sins of your family; pray for the true Reign of the Sacred Heart in your home, with all the graces that flow therefrom.

Jesus, pleading:

You have done well in anticipating my wish by speaking of those whom I love so much because you, My consoling angel, love them. Know that your home is Mine also, and this notwithstanding its failings which you and I regret. I bless it with all My Heart and I shall watch over your dear ones and shower My graces on them in order to repay this vigil of contrite love and reparation. Ah, and more! You shall know one day all that you have done for them by sacrificing your sleep in order to give Me consolation in this hour of darkness and sin. Confide to Me, then, the troubles of your home, all that worries you, and be at peace; I am watching over it.

But do not forget that I am the Divine Outcast of many, many homes —pray for them. Oh, how grave a crime is that of the unfaithful home! To profane it is to profane the first of My sanctuaries, that never-to-be-forgotten Nazareth, whose altar was the heart of My Immaculate Mother. Alas, how many are the homes which do not deserve that sacred name, homes from which I am expelled by a life of sin.

In the name of a false progress the foundation of the domestic sanctuary has been undermined. The bond of Christian marriage has been profaned and sacrilegiously broken; it has been robbed of its beauty and its divine greatness. That has been horribly "humanized" which I had made divine: conjugal love and its fruitfulness.

And as if so much ruin and desolation were not enough, there is now the whirlwind of an actual pagan regeneration, the perversion of morals, the excessive liberty of the young, the dreadful frivolity of the Christian woman and her provocative immodesty. That throng of evils, all grave, is the avalanche which threatens to bury the little that still survives of dignity and Christian virtue.

Beloved soul, pray, make reparation, placate My justice, and obtain, instead of rigorous chastisement, mercy, which will be granted in consideration of a phalanx of souls who, like you, love and immolate themselves in order to rescue the guilty world.

And now call to your aid the Queen of Nazareth, My Mother, who grieves desolate with Me over so many ruins and scandals. Adoring soul, call upon her who comes to help you stay the arm of My justice by holding back the torrent of iniquity which outrages Me; invoke her because she, the sweet Nazarene, is the great Reparatrix — she it is who with you is saving the menaced family.

The adoring soul:

O Mary, Star of the Sea, come to our aid and save the work and the property of thy Jesus, because Nazareth — the home is found to be in great peril. Mother of God, save us!

Hear me, O my Queen and my Mother, for this concerns the very throne of our Savior. Alas, the generation of true Christian mothers is all but spent; the Christian home is dying out. Mother of God, save us!

What a horror! The fountain of human and divine life is about to dry up because there are so many worldly wives who disdain and even dread the honor of motherhood. Mother of God, save us!

And alas, that youth which ought to be a future in flower is a fading flower, without the sap of purity or of virtue. Mother of God, save us!

And those little ones! Oh, what a grief that, awakening to life in the midst of moral corruption and scorched by the sudden blaze of a worldly home, they are no longer children! Mother of God, save us!

Queen of Martyrs and Mother of Sorrows, only thou and Jesus know and comprehend fully the depths of these evils and of others that have not been named. By thy tears, by the seven swords which pierced thy soul, by the weary, anguished sighs of Jesus, by His agony and thine own, O Mediatrix of Mercy, come and save us! Save the family, the cornerstone of the Reign of thy Child, the Divine King.

O Mary, return to the home as its Queen, impregnate it anew with the perfume of thy virtues —thou, the Lily of Paradise — embalm it with the fragrance of chastity; rebuild Nazareth and Bethany, and be once more our life, our sweetness and our hope"!

Mary, save the family for Jesus! Jesus, save the family through Mary!

Say the Hail, holy Queen to obtain the Reign of the Sacred Heart in the home.

The voice of Jesus, pleading:

Atoning soul, listen to Me with a loving, docile heart, for I must confide to you something very great which superficial Christians are not capable of understanding. But first of all invoke My Mother; say with fervor a Hail Mary in order that My words may penetrate with divine light into your heart. Hail Mary. . . .

Tell Me, dear child, do you love with a great love and venerate with great devotion, My august Vicar, the Pope? Have you realized that, after Mary, the Pope is the greatest gift of My Sacred Heart?

Through Mary Immaculate I gave Myself to the world; through My infallible Vicar I make known to it My Will and My law. He is a never-failing proof of My love; he is My oracle and My voice. He is My right hand and My divine power here on earth, and so it shall be until the end of the world. I have placed in his heart My Divine Heart —therefore is he Father and Pontiff!

The Holy Ghost hovers over him as over the Apostles in the Cenacle, and My Mother, through

My special commission, watches over him as My Prime Minister and Vicar.

Although I am silent in the tabernacle, I speak in the Vatican in exile; in both I am always your Lord and King.

Oh, what sorrow that so many children of My Church offend Me cruelly by offending the Pope; it is I Myself Whom they wound when they boldly indulge in mad criticism against him.

And more, when they refuse to heed his counsels and cast aside his norms, it is I Whom they are disobeying, for if he is the mouthpiece I am the Voice.

But what shall I say of those who would dare outrage his person, which is Mine? That a child of My own should strike My face, which is that of the Pontiff of Rome!

Pray and make reparation, for I assure you that there are many who are damning themselves in this hurricane of rebellion. Think how I have invested My Vicar with full authority to bind and loose, to guide and govern, to prescribe and prohibit in My name. All power has been conferred on him.

I assure you of this, My beloved adorer: many, very many are the souls who find themselves on the brink of an abyss because they are not submissive to the Successor of Peter.

Look at that innumerable host of wretched women whose immodest dress My Vicar has condemned over and over again, but who, in their disobedience and rebellion, continue to sow the seed of scandal. Shall I have to curse them?

And there you have those men, puffed up with pride, who on their own account have set themselves up as masters and doctors over Christian Society without any other claim than that of their self-conceit, for they know full well that on no one, absolutely no one, have I conferred infallible power save on the Pope, the Bishop of Rome. Shall I, likewise, have to curse them?

And how many others there are who do not accept the pronouncements of My Vicar except insofar as it pleases them or suits their fancy to do so; who interpret his definite decisions in their own fashion and refuse obedience according to the Catholic spirit.

If you but knew, beloved soul, how I am wounded by such an attitude, so un-Catholic because so lacking in filial respect and humility. How many griefs and what deceptions I receive, where you least imagine, in this grave and delicate matter!

You who desire to make reparation, restrain these souls on such a dangerous downward path — perhaps the most dangerous of all — and give Me the glory and joy of seeing the Supreme Pontiff deeply loved and respected, filially obeyed and venerated. For you must know and make known that whosoever honors and loves him honors Me, and by this filial love enraptures My Heart!

The adoring soul:

Thank Thee, my Jesus, for the lesson Thou hast just given me concerning him who represents Thee visibly on this earth. And let me tell Thee first of all, O King of Love, that if I have ever offended Thee by not giving to Thy august Vicar the love, the veneration and the filial obedience which Thou dost expect of me, on my knees I ask Thy pardon a thousand times! To make reparation for this fault and to dry the tears which, because of it, run down Thy holy face, I offer myself in union with the Host of the Mass for the intentions of the Holy Father. Graciously hear me, O Lord.

O Mary, Queen of the Church and of the Cenacle, through thy Immaculate Heart I offer and consecrate to the Sacred Heart of Jesus all my sufferings of heart, mind and body, in reparation for the open rebellion against the Sovereign Pontiff. Obtain pardon for that sin, and mercy and light for those sinners!

O Mary, Queen of the Church and of the Cenacle, through thy Immaculate Heart I offer and consecrate all my Spiritual Communions, which I desire should be most fervent, in reparation for the criticisms and the distrustful, irreverent attitude by which the dignity of the Holy Father is offended. Obtain pardon for that sin, and mercy and light for those sinners!

I thank Thee, Heart of Jesus, for that gift of Thy love which is, for us Catholics, the Pope, in whom Thou hast desired to leave us, a thousand times better than in the relic of the Holy Shroud, not only a vestige but the living reflection of Thy Adorable Person. For this, in the name of all faithful Catholics and likewise in the name of many who do not know or who disown this incomparable gift of Thy goodness, I praise Thee, together with all the martyrs of our Faith, and I bless Thee in union with the confessors and apostles of all times, who have fought and won in the shadow of the Cross and under obedience to the Roman Pontiff.

And thou, St. Thérèse, "Little Flower of Jesus," who hast loved the Church and the Pope so much, thou who didst offer thyself as a victim of love for the exaltation of our Holy Mother the Church, and whose apostolic mission has been solemnly confirmed by the Vicar of Christ: draw anew to the fold many prodigals, cause them to recognize the supreme authority of such a Shepherd and Father, the "sweet visible Christ" who is the Pope. O St. Therese, hasten the triumph of the Church and shower down your heavenly roses on our Holy Father.

Say the Hail, Holy Queen for the Pope, and promise always to pray for him, to love him and to obey him with filial affection, for in the heart of the Pope we ought to see the Heart of Christ.

Read the following very slowly, relishing its spiritual sweetness, as if you heard the voice of Jesus, broken by His sobs and moans.

Jesus, pleading:

Hear Me, beloved soul. It was not only, nor principally, Pilate and the Sanhedrin who condemned Me. Oh, no! It was the world — as much and even more guilty than they. That is why I said, and I repeat, that "I pray not for the world."

Imagine how I suffer in seeing so many of My children, and among them those most loved and favored by Me, become completely worldly-minded. What a sorrow! I assure you that far more cruel than the outrage of the wicked is this other outrage which pierces My Heart: that of beloved souls who have actually abandoned Me by compromising with the world and consequently robbing My Heart.

Kiss with tenderness, atoning soul, kiss with sorrow and emotion, the Five Wounds of your crucifix, and say: "Mercy, O Sacred Heart of Jesus, mercy! I love Thee, my Lord and my King, for all those ungrateful ones, and in reparation I promise eternal fidelity to Thy law. Thy Kingdom come!"

Jesus:

Adoring soul, hear My groans, weep with Me, and let Me confide to you the fearful agony which is surging in My Heart. I am constrained to unburden My grief to you.

Behold, in the distance there, that great and frivolous crowd! Do you hear how they laugh, how they sing and dance with mad merriment? It is Balthasar's prophetic banquet over again — the crazed rapture of pleasure which often precedes, scarcely by a few hours, an eternity of woe. You who love Me, share My tears, mourn over this guilty folly, make reparation.

Kiss with immense love the Five Wounds of your crucifix, and say: "Mercy, O Sacred Heart of Jesus, mercy! I love Thee, my Lord and my King, for all those ungrateful ones, and in reparation I promise eternal fidelity to Thy law. Thy Kingdom come!"

Jesus:

Count, if you can, beloved soul, the army of frivolous and worldly ones of our day, of those who live feverish, giddy lives in pleasures and sinful diversions. They have profaned their senses, even though their bodies were consecrated to Me through Baptism and the Holy Eucharist. See how My wounds bleed, reopened by these wretched ones! Do you, at least, O atoning soul, weep with Me over so great a sin, such folly, and make reparation for it.

Kiss with loving sorrow the Five Wounds of your crucifix, and say: "Mercy, O Sacred Heart of Jesus, mercy! I love Thee, my Lord and my King, for all those ungrateful ones, and in reparation I promise eternal fidelity to Thy law. Thy Kingdom come!"

Jesus:

Alas, contemplate — but from a distance, in order that thou mayest not be contaminated — those theatres and places of worldly amusement, television and internet. Ah, Roman soldiers once 'gave Me gall for My drink, but a far more bitter draught is prepared for Me today! For those men and women, those young boys and girls whom you see, and who have paid a luxury price to witness these sinful spectacles, wickedly con-sidered a necessity and a matter of progress in this age — these very persons have approached the communion-rail, perhaps frequently. Oh, what a suffering! And they call themselves Mine!

Accursed scenes of impurity, where the sin of the flesh is exhibited with a satanic refinement that scourges Me on the face and cuts into My Sacred Heart with bitterness! Do you, at least, O atoning soul, weep with Me over so great a sin, over such folly, and make reparation for it.

Kiss with loving sorrow the Five Wounds of your crucifix, and say: "Mercy, O Sacred Heart of Jesus, mercy! I love Thee, my Lord and my King, for all those ungrateful ones, and in reparation I promise eternal fidelity to Thy law. Thy Kingdom come!"(A brief pause to beg for pardon.)

Jesus:

My sorrow is turned into an agony! Look at those women whom My Immaculate Mother rescued from an abyss of slavery and abjection, and then, at My request, adopted as her children that she might adorn them with the angelic beauty of chastity and enrich them with the treasures of purity and Christian virtue. Behold how they have trampled underfoot all the laws of modesty and womanly refinement, how they have disfigured and sullied the Christian beauty of their sex. Oh, what a sin!

But do not look at these unworthy Christians. Lest you be contaminated, do not look at these sowers of sin on the streets or even in church. Close your eyes, as I do, for these Christians are My dishonor.

Ah, I grieve, and My Mother with Me. But among many today, Venus the goddess of worldlings triumphs insolently while I am set aside, because the trappings of vanity are, in their eyes, worth more than My Person and My law. O wretched ones!

From you, atoning soul, I, a God torn by scourges, beg for compassion and consolation, for My executioners are these fashionably dressed women with beautiful hands, who by scourging Me with their immodesty have lashed My divine flesh to pieces.

Do you, My consoling angel, remove this chalice from Me. Weep with Me over so great a sin, over such folly, and make reparation for it.

Kiss with loving sorrow the Five Wounds of your crucifix, and say: "Mercy, O Sacred Heart of Jesus, mercy! I love Thee, my Lord and my King, for all those ungrateful ones, and in reparation I promise eternal fidelity to Thy law. Thy Kingdom come!"

The young are growing up like those poisonous plants that spring up on the borders of a swamp: they grow while carrying already in their veins the germ of death.

And so many women who have been baptized but are otherwise not Christians, languish and wither away to the sound of modern dance music, which in reality is sounding a funeral tone, announcing, with the death of their souls, the death and the ruin of the Christian home. Ah yes, see how the family, the sacred home-nest of tender affections, of fruitfulness and of peace, is seriously threatened with disruption and death.

Yet we know that Jesus Himself formed the sanctuary of the Christian home in Nazareth; for this He raised up and ennobled all womanhood in Mary; and to consolidate this divine work He poured out His Precious Blood, because He willed to civilize and Christianize us.

Ah, poor, poor Jesus! See His cherished and favored children, see how they are destroying His work while making Him taste the vinegar and gall of their sin. Yet His Sacred Heart, patient and meek, waits for them, offering pardon and love!

The adoring soul:

O Jesus, Life of my life, my God and my All, my King and my Savior, in spirit I kiss with tenderness and with immense sorrow the whips of

Thy executioners, in order to make reparation for
the scourging inflicted on Thee nowadays by every
impure soul and especially by immodest women.
I love Thee, O Jesus, even unto folly. I love Thee
because Thou art Jesus!

O Jesus, Life of my life, let me in spirit kiss the
nails which pierced Thy divine flesh, in order to
make reparation for the countless scandals which
are promoted and even paid for by many Catholics,
seduced as they are by a world that is suffering from
the dreadful fever of sensuality. I love Thee, O Jesus,
even unto folly. I love Thee because Thou art Jesus!

O Jesus, Life of my life, with tenderness and
sorrow I kiss the Cross, Thy blood-stained throne,
from which amid the spasms of Thy agony Thou
didst see with bitterest grief all that is happening
today, all that believers and Christians are permitting
themselves on the pretense of social requirements
and modern progress, and which at bottom is
nothing but the degradation of woman and the
rebellion of proud man. From this glorified Cross
Thou wilt one day pronounce a final malediction on
the lovers of this world and wilt judge them with the
awful rigor which they themselves have provoked,

because they would not accept and live by Thy law of sanctity and of mercy. Have pity, O Adorable Lawgiver and King; have pity, most amiable Savior! O Jesus, I love Thee even unto folly, because Thou art Jesus!

Say this ejaculation five times in a spirit of atonement: O Jesus, I love Thee even unto folly, because Thou art Jesus!

Reflection

Make here a brief examination of conscience. Have you not perhaps likewise yielded to the sinful demands of the world? to its crazed vanities? in the matter of amusements, reading, shows and dances? as regards immodest fashions? when frequenting public beaches? have you nothing with which to reproach yourself? nothing at all? Think this over seriously now, before the tribunal of pardon and mercy, with the strong resolution of changing and of making reparation for that which today causes a justified remorse. Remember that otherwise you will one day see it with noonday clearness and with terror, but before an implacable tribunal, and all too late.

Consider that since Jesus, your Divine Master, has condemned the world, no Christian is able to or ought to accept its maxims, its spirit of pride and sensuality, which are the very negation of the Gospel and of the Christian law.

Make an act of contrition as firm and sincere as if this were your last hour.

And now, like St. John, leaning your head in spirit on the Heart of Jesus, listen to His tender complaints, to His pleas for love and reparation.

The voice of Jesus, pleading:

Beloved soul, your vocation is to love, to love Me!

Oh, love Me with your whole heart, with your whole soul, and with all your strength, since I have created you solely for this end: to love Me and to be loved by Me in time and in eternity.

I thirst! I am consumed with thirst for the love of My own! And My own deny Me this love, they rob My Heart. See how they love all that is noble and worthy: family, friends, benefactors, country —but in lavishing so much love on all others, they have forgotten Me, Who am none else but the God of Love! What more can I do to win them to My Sacred Heart? What new prodigies can I perform when I have spent Myself in giving My own Self to these ungrateful children? Can anyone conceive of a charity more sublime than that of a God Who gives Himself to His own? Is not this already the gift of Paradise? Ah, but see how in return they give Me coldness, indifference, forgetfulness and frequently even sin and ingratitude.

I thirst! I have an immense thirst, a devouring thirst of being loved by My own!

Listen to Me, adoring soul. If only, at least as reparation for the many crimes which renew My Passion — after being scourged by the scandals of the theatre, of indecent fashions and of the infamous beaches — if only, as satisfaction for this over-flowing of pride, of vanity and of impurity, I might find many generous souls who would console Me with love and penance — but there are so few!

Oh, the sorrow of it! This holy desire for loving reparation is growing less every day. How few are those who truly know how to give themselves to Me, with genuine rejection of the perverted maxims of the world! What coldness in the hearts of those who call themselves Mine! How little loyalty toward Me! Alas, they do not love Me!

Do you, at least, place your lips and your heart on the wound in My pierced side and tell Me — Oh, tell

Me that you love Me. Kiss the Sacred Wound on your crucifix, putting your whole soul into that kiss, and saying five times: "I love Thee, O Jesus, Love Who art not loved! Inflame and consume my heart in Thy divine charity"

Jesus:

Thank you, beloved soul, thank you! How you comfort My Heart and lessen My thirst by speaking to Me thus! But, hear Me further.

Since I, with sadness, begged My servant Margaret Mary for more love of the Holy Eucharist a homage of reparation, the number of Eucharistic souls has indeed increased, but they are still a restricted group. And even more limited is the number of those who have understood that it is not enough to receive Holy Communion, it is necessary to love in communicating. Otherwise there is the danger that this incomparable gift of the altar might begin to pall. For to assist at the Holy Sacrifice of the Mass without great love and to receive Holy Communion without truly giving Me your heart, is to fail to recognize the love which has created these marvels and to hinder in great part their efficacy.

That which I have given out of pure love ought to be received and repaid with immense love. It is not enough to participate in the Banquet, it is necessary to draw near with a divine hunger for the Bread of Life.

Happy are you, adoring soul, that you understand this language which so many others fail to understand because they do not love. And it is precisely because they do not love that I am abandoned and left utterly alone in My tabernacles. Yet how many crowds, what multitudes, there are in the market places of sin, while I in My little dwelling of the tabernacle am always alone!

There are not lacking, of course, those friends of formality: the many who worship Me with their lips but whose hearts are far from Me.

Oh, how many friends have I sought out, who do not seek for Me — friends to whom I have given Myself, but who do not give themselves to Me —friends most faithful and self-sacrificing with their worldly friends, but not with Me, their Lord and Savior —friends who even to an imprudent extent confide in creatures, always self-interested, but who will not trust in Me nor give themselves to My Sacred Heart, always faithful!

Alas, yes, how many there are who know how to sacrifice themselves nobly for a cause that is beautiful, but only human — for a creature, good perhaps, but yet a creature — and who do not give to Me a hundredth part of this nobleness, of this sacrifice: who refuse it to Me because they are always afraid of exaggerating where My Adorable Person is concerned! Friends without any zeal for My glory, friends who seek Me with eagerness when they have need of My miracles, but never when I seek an hour of their time or self-sacrifice for My glory!

What am I to think of these ungrateful ones who pretend to love Me because they pray and even dare to communicate, but whose vanity, whose immodesty in dress, whose worldly frivolity have opened an impassable abyss between their hearts and Mine? Such souls as these deceive themselves, but they do not deceive Me.

I do not accept — I reject indignantly — this artificial devotion of prayers and novenas that bear no fruit of amendment, this false devotion which pretends to unite what I have separated forever: My law and virtue, My love and My Heart, from the world which I again curse. What surprises these "devout worldlings" will receive at My judgment seat!

I have a divine hunger for really loving hearts: not for beautiful words, nor for flowers and hymns and empty prayers.

I thirst for a love that is trustful and self-sacrificing and humble, for a love that is pure of soul and chaste in the senses. To give Me any other love in league with the world, would be to lie to oneself and to Me. I reject it!

The love that is strong as death is what I expect from you, adoring soul. Oh, give it to Me, quench the thirst of a God Who came down from Heaven to seek the love of His poor creatures. And since so many hearts, alas, are to Me as a dry cistern, unable to give the living water which I give and which I hope for as a return of love, do you give Me to drink.

I thirst — I thirst for love!

Read the following very slowly, speaking to Jesus more with your heart than with your lips. The adoring soul:

O my agonizing King, if Thine "I thirst" on Calvary brought vinegar and gall to Thy divine lips, tonight Thou art going to receive the sweetness of honey and nectar which my poor heart offers Thee in reparation. Listen to me, most loving Jesus!

Infinite Love Who art not loved, I love Thee and I desire to make Thee loved, in reparation for so many who have failed to recognize that prodigy of Thy love which is Thy marvelous Incarnation. Jesus the Infant, Jesus the Youth, Jesus the Divine Workman, I adore Thee with the adoration of the heart. But in return do Thou inflame this poor heart of mine in the flames of Thy charity. "O that I might love Thee as Thou hast never yet been loved!" And give me Thy Heart, give me Thy love, for I too thirst, I thirst ardently for Thee, Lord Jesus. I thirst!

Infinite Love Who art not loved, I love Thee and I desire to make Thee loved, in reparation for so many who have failed to recognize in their lives that folly of divine love which is Thy Passion, Thy Redemption and Thy Cross. Jesus crucified, Jesus agonizing, Jesus dead and buried for love's sake, I adore Thee with the adoration of the heart. But in return do Thou inflame this poor heart of mine in the flames of Thy charity. "O that I might love Thee as Thou hast never yet been loved!" And give me Thy Heart, give me Thy love, for I too thirst,' I thirst ardently for Thee, Lord Jesus. I thirst!

Infinite Love Who art not loved, I love Thee and I desire to make Thee loved, in reparation for so many who have failed to recognize that divine folly of love which is the Most Holy Sacrament of the Altar. Jesus our Priest, Jesus our Victim, Jesus our Sacramental Food, I love Thee with the adoration of the heart. But in return do Thou inflame this poor heart of mine in the flames of Thy charity. "O that I might love Thee as Thou hast never yet been loved!" And give me Thy Heart, give me Thy love, for I too thirst, I thirst ardently for Thee, Lord Jesus. I thirst!

Grant that I may love Thee, O Jesus, Love Who art not loved, that I may love Thee in my personal and intimate life, by perfect fidelity to Thy grace —that I may sanctify myself in Thy love.

Grant that I may love Thee, O Jesus, Love Who art not loved, that I may love Thee in my family life, in the exact fulfillment of my daily duties and in the acceptance of those crosses connected with my state of life and permitted by Thy loving Providence —that I may sanctify myself in Thy love.

Grant that I may love Thee, O Jesus, Love Who art not loved, that I may love Thee in the souls whom Thou hast committed to my care, especially in those who have gone astray. Grant that I may love Thee in my apostolate for Thy glory and, that it may be fruitful, let me sanctify myself in Thy love. Grant that I may love Thee, O Jesus, Love Who art not loved, in Thine ineffable gift of the heart of Mary, that in this school I may learn to be simple, humble, chaste and pure — that guided by Mary, I may sanctify myself in Thy love.

Ah, how much I desire, dear Jesus, that my life might be a perfect praise of Thine unknown love, a reparation for Thy offended love, a holocaust to Thy despised and profaned love. But Thou, O Lord, Who knowest all things, Who readest the depths of souls and Who dost see my immense desires: Thou knowest that in spite of my miseries I desire with a resolute will to live and to die saying and proving to Thee that I love Thee above all the treasures of Heaven and earth. I thirst for Thee, O Jesus! I thirst for Thy glory!

Act of Reparation to the Sacred Heart

ACT OF REPARATION TO THE
MOST SACRED HEART OF JESUS

By His Holiness, Pius XI

O sweet Jesus, Whose overflowing charity for men is requited by so much forgetfulness, negligence and contempt, behold us prostrate before Thine altar, eager to repair by a special act of homage the cruel indifference and injuries to which Thy loving Heart is everywhere subject.

Mindful, alas, that we ourselves have had a share in those great indignities which we now deplore from the depths of our hearts, we humbly ask Thy pardon and declare our readiness to atone by voluntary expiation not only for our own personal offenses, but also for the sins of those who, straying far from the path of salvation, refuse in their obstinate infidelity to follow Thee, their Shepherd and Leader, or who, renouncing the vows of their Baptism, have cast off the sweet yoke of Thy law.

We are now resolved to expiate each and every outrage committed against Thee; we are determined to make amends for the manifold offenses against Christian modesty in unbecoming dress and behavior, for all the foul seductions laid to ensnare the feet of the innocent, for the frequent violation of Sundays and holydays, and the shocking blasphemies uttered against Thee and Thy saints. We wish also to make amends for the insults to which Thy Vicar on earth and Thy priests are subjected; for the profanation, by conscious neglect or terrible acts of sacrilege, of the very Sacrament of Thy divine love;

and lastly for the public crimes of nations who resist the rights and the teaching authority of the Church which Thou hast founded.

Would, O Divine Jesus, we were able to wash away such abominations with our blood. We now offer, in reparation for these violations of Thy divine honor, the satisfaction Thou didst once make to Thine Eternal Father on the Cross and which Thou dost continue daily on our altars; we offer it in union with the acts of atonement of Thy Virgin Mother, of all the saints and of the pious faithful on earth; and we sincerely promise to make recompense, as far as we can with the help of Thy grace, for all neglect of Thy great love and for the sins we and others have committed in the past. Henceforth we will live a life of unwavering faith, of purity of conduct, and of perfect observance of the precepts of the Gospel, especially that of charity. We promise to the best of our power to prevent others from offending Thee and to bring as many as possible to follow Thee.

O loving Jesus, through the intercession of the Blessed Virgin Mary, our model in reparation, deign to receive the voluntary offering we make of this act of expiation; and by the crowning gift of perseverance keep us faithful unto death in our duty and the allegiance we owe to Thee, so that we may all one day come to that happy home where Thou with the Father and the Holy Ghost livest and reignest God, world without end. Amen.

And now, adoring soul, take your crucifix and with immense love kiss the Five Wounds, saying each time the following ejaculation: "I love Thee, O Jesus, because Thou art Jesus! Thy Kingdom come!"

Kiss the Wound in the Sacred Side of Jesus, praying for the intentions of the Holy Father, and say: "I love Thee, O Jesus, because Thou art Jesus! Thy Kingdom come!"

Kiss the Right Hand of our Crucified Savior, praying for bishops, priests and seminarians, and say: "I love Thee, O Jesus, because Thou art Jesus! Thy Kingdom come!"

Kiss the Left Hand of our Crucified Savior, praying for your family and your own personal needs, and say: "I love Thee, O Jesus, because Thou art Jesus! Thy Kingdom come!"

Kiss the Right Foot of our Crucified Savior, as the apostle of His love, praying for the triumph of His Sacred Heart, and say: "I love Thee, O Jesus, because Thou art Jesus! Thy Kingdom come!"

Kiss the Left Foot of our Crucified Savior, praying for the conversion of sinners and those who have gone astray, and say: "I love Thee, O Jesus, because Thou art Jesus! Thy Kingdom come!"

The adoring soul:

In taking leave of Thee tonight, O King of Love, Heart of my God and God of my heart, I enter confidently through that wound caused by my sins, into the ark of divine and infinite tenderness which is Thy loving Heart. And here will I stay forever, to repeat to Thee through all time that I love Thee and long to make Thee loved — and to sing throughout Eternity the infinite mercies of Thy Sacred Heart.

Act of Consecration to the Sacred Heart

ACT OF CONSECRATION TO THE MOST SACRED HEART OF JESUS

By His Holiness, Leo XIII

Most sweet Jesus, Redeemer of the human race, look down upon us humbly prostrate before Thy altar. We are Thine and Thine we wish to be; but to be more surely united with Thee, behold, each one of us freely consecrates himself today to

Thy Most Sacred Heart. Many indeed have never known Thee; many, too, despising Thy precepts, have rejected Thee. Have mercy on them all, most merciful Jesus, and draw them to Thy Sacred Heart. Be Thou King, O Lord, not only of the faithful who have never forsaken Thee, but also of the prodigal children who have abandoned Thee; grant that they may quickly return to their Father's house lest they die of wretchedness and hunger. Be Thou King of those who are deceived by erroneous opinions or whom discord keeps aloof, and call them back to the harbor of truth and unity of faith, so that soon there may be but one flock and one Shepherd. Be Thou King also of all those who are still involved in the darkness of idolatry or of Islamism, and refuse not to deliver them out of darkness into the light and the Kingdom of God. Turn Thine eyes of mercy toward the children of that race, once Thy chosen people. Of old they called down upon themselves the Blood of the Savior; may it now descend upon them a laver of redemption and of life. Grant, O Lord, to Thy Church assurance of freedom and immunity from harm, give peace and order to all nations, and make the earth resound from pole to pole with one cry: Praise to the Divine Heart that wrought our salvation; to it be glory and honor forever. Amen.

As an act of adoration and reparation let us say five times, in honor of the Five Wounds: "Most Sacred Heart of Jesus, Thy Kingdom come!"

Prayer for the Conversions of Heretics & Schismatics & All Non-Catholics

O Mary, Mother of mercy and Refuge of sinners, we beseech thee, be pleased to look with pitiful eyes upon poor heretics and schismatics. Thou who art the Seat of Wisdom, enlighten the minds that are miserably enfolded in the darkness of ignorance and sin, that they may clearly know that

the Holy Catholic and Apostolic Roman Church
is the one true Church of Jesus Christ, outside of
which neither holiness nor salvation can be found.

Finish the work of their conversion by obtaining
for them the grace to accept all the truths of our
Holy Faith, and to submit themselves to the supreme
Roman Pontiff, the Vicar of Jesus Christ on earth;
that so, being united with us in the sweet chains
of divine charity, there may soon be only one fold
under the same one shepherd; and may we all, O
glorious Virgin, sing forever with exultation: Rejoice,
O Virgin Mary, thou only hast destroyed all heresies
in the whole world. Amen.

Hail Mary, three times.

An Indulgence of 500 days (S.C. Prop. of the
Faith., Dec. 30, 1868;S.P. Ap., March 18, 1936.
Raccolta No. 579).

Regulations & Indulgences

The Night Adorer promises to make one hour of adoration once a month during the night. The night begins with the hour from 9 to 10 p. m., and ends with the hour from 5 to 6 a. m. Adoration made at any other time is meritorious but is not sufficient to gain the indulgences.

As an act of generosity, Night Adorers are encouraged to leave the choice of their date and hour of adoration to the Director, but are perfectly free to choose their own date and hour for any reasonable motive. Any date and hour of the month may be selected, either a fixed date such as the fifteenth of each month, or a movable date such as the First Friday.

In order to keep accurate records and to maintain continuous nights of adoration, deaths and withdrawals of members, as well as changes of address, should be made known to the Promoter, or to the Center where names are registered.

It is not necessary to renew the enrollment each year. Once enrolled, you continue to be a member until death or voluntary withdrawal.

The promise you make does not bind under pain of sin, even venial. Father Mateo started Night Adoration in the Home as an act of loving homage and reparation to the Sacred Heart. Accordingly, its success and duration will depend upon the extent of the faithfulness and generosity of the members. This fidelity will be proved when, prevented by sickness or other disability from taking your usual time, you make your hour of adoration some other night. It is not necessary to notify the Director of temporary change of date or hour.

INDULGENCES

By decree of April 27, 1929, the Very Reverend
Father General of the Franciscan Fathers affiliated
the League of Night Adoration to this Order, and
granted all Night Adorers participation in its merits.
On May 17, 1929, the League of Night Adoration
was affiliated to the Franciscan Confraternity of
Nocturnal Reparation in Italy. This was ratified
by the Sacred Congregation of the Council by
a Rescript of April 14, 1930. By virtue of this
affiliation, the members of the League can gain the
following indulgences.

a) A PLENARY INDULGENCE on the Usual
Conditions

b) A PLENARY INDULGENCE at the hour of
death if the members, having received the Sacraments
of Penance and Holy Eucharist, or at least, being
contrite, invoke the holy name of Jesus — if possible
with their lips, otherwise in their heart — and
patiently accept death as coming from the hand of
God and as the wages of sin.

c) A PARTIAL INDULGENCE of 7 years for
every extra hour of adoration made with a contrite
heart.